Original title:
Sapling Stories

Copyright © 2025 Creative Arts Management OÜ
All rights reserved.

Author: Adrian Caldwell
ISBN HARDBACK: 978-1-80567-276-0
ISBN PAPERBACK: 978-1-80567-575-4

Dreaming in the Dappled Light

In the glade where shadows play,
Little creatures chase the day.
Leaves that giggle in the breeze,
Whispers float through tall oak trees.

Sunbeams dance on tiny feet,
While squirrels scamper, oh so fleet.
A ladybug wears polka dots,
Making friends with the sun-kissed knots.

From Acorn to Oak

An acorn dreams of skies so blue,
Wonders what a tree can do.
'Tomorrow I'll stretch very tall!'
But first, must dodge the squirrel's call.

Beneath the ground, a tale unfolds,
Roots whisper secrets, brave and bold.
'I'll grow so big, it's hard to doubt!'
Then trips on worms, oh what a rout!

Fluttering Leaves and Hope

Leaves like paper, all aglow,
Tell the stories we don't know.
Winds tickle them with a tease,
They flutter down with laugh and ease.

Each flurry spins a silly dance,
As critters join in, take a chance.
A rhyme escapes from bark so wise,
'These giggles wear the brightest ties!'

The Journey of the Young Seed

A seed woke up from winter's sleep,
Said, 'I'm off, the world's to reap!'
It rolled and tumbled, went on a spree,
Challenged a rock to a race, whee!

With sun above and dirt below,
Befriended ants, 'Hey, let's go slow!'
Together they laughed, made a parade,
All while dreaming of leafy shade.

A Journey in Each Sprout

In the garden, little green,
A tiny sprout, what a scene!
Wiggled its roots, wanting to roam,
Said, "I'll grow up far from home!"

But oh! A bird perched above,
Singing tales of dirt and love.
"Stay close, my friend, you'll surely see,
You'll be a tree, just wait for me!"

The Breath of Life

Whispered secrets, soft and light,
A leaf giggles in morning light.
"I'm green and spry, that's quite a feat,
What do you think of my leafy seat?"

A breeze replied with playful ease,
"Your roots are tickled by the tease!
Let's dance around, sway and twirl,
You'll sprout some joy in this great whirl!"

Tales in the Breeze

A playful wind began to speak,
Tales of trees and flowers unique.
"Just yesterday I saw a seed,
Wearing shoes and dancing with speed!"

Off to the park, it rolled away,
Inviting bugs for a grand ballet.
"Oh, how they twirled, such a sight!
Even the worms grooved with delight!"

Sheltered Dreams

In cozy shade, a sprout took a nap,
Dreaming of adventures, oh what a flap!
"Today, I'll surf on a leaf, oh joy!
Then I'll beat a drum made of soil, oh boy!"

But suddenly rain began to pour,
"Not again! I'm stuck in a chore!"
Yet puddles formed, a splashy delight,
"Who knew such wet things could feel so right?"

Stories in Every Ring

In the garden, a sprout takes a peek,
Whispers to the worms about the unique.
Its leaves dance lightly, a jolly old jig,
'Tell me your secrets,' it nudges a pig.

Time rolls like marbles, the rings grow wide,
Each year a chapter, they swell with pride.
The tales of windstorms and sunlit delight,
Make every tree laugh on a starry night.

A Canopy of Wishes

Up high in the leaves, the dreams take flight,
A squirrel with wishes sings to the night.
He juggles acorns, a comical scene,
While hoping for rainbows, if you know what I mean.

The branches reach out, with a tickle and tease,
They whisper to clouds, 'Please bring us some breeze.'
Each plump little fruit holds a giggle inside,
Waiting for children to come and confide.

Conversations between Roots

Under the soil, the roots share a brew,
Gossiping softly, oh, what a crew!
One root says, 'Did you hear 'bout the tree?
It's thinking of growing a new hip marquee!'

They chuckle and wiggle in moist, darkened earth,
Pondering which sprout will have the most girth.
With whispers of rain and a jest here and there,
Roots share their dreams in the cool underground air.

Emergence from Earth

With a wiggle and squirm, the sprouts push on through,
Eager to greet all the sunlight so new.
'Excuse me, dear soil,' one small sprout cries,
'I'm ready for laughter, let's reach for the skies!'

The earth shakes with giggles, as flowers all bloom,
Dancing around, like they're stuck in a room.
Every bud has a story, a joke to unfold,
In this garden of mirth, the laughter won't fold.

Nature's Tender Resolutes

In a world where leaves wear hats,
The ants throw parties on the mats.
Grasshoppers dance, with no regrets,
While daisies gossip 'bout their pets.

A squirrel with a treasure chest,
Claims it's nuts, but it's a quest.
He's busy plotting in the trees,
With acorn maps and cozy teas.

The sun winks down, a playful tease,
While clouds mumble, 'Let's take it easy!'
The daisies twirl in sunny glee,
While bumblebees sing, "Whee! Whee! Whee!"

In nature's kitchen, a mix of fun,
With spicy winds and laughing sun.
The whole wide world is just a game,
And each new sprout has found its fame.

Spirals of Life

A snail in slippers on a path,
Scratched a joke, and caused a laugh.
He said, 'Why rush? I'm on a roll!'
And all the cacti lost control.

The trees had trunks like funny hats,
With raccoons acting like acrobats.
They swung and flipped from vine to vine,
While mushrooms mimicked a dance divine.

The wind made whistles, soft and sweet,
Twirling leaves like they're on their feet.
The earth below giggled in delight,
As every critter joined the flight.

In spirals twirling, life unfolds,
With silly moments to behold.
Each loop a chuckle, any twist a grin,
In nature's dance — we all dive in!

Buds and Blossoms

A bud turned blossom in the sun,
Said, 'I'm ready, let's have some fun!'
With petals bright and fragrance sweet,
She danced along with roots and feet.

The bees wore costumes, all a-buzz,
While ladybugs played hopscotch fuzz.
The daisies groaned, 'Oh what a mess!
We'd join, but we're a bit too dressed!'

Chickadees chirped a merry tune,
While butterflies got lost too soon.
They whispered secret jokes in flight,
Creating giggles, pure delight.

In emerald fields where antics play,
Every bloom has something to say.
And nature smiles, a jester bold,
In stories of joy yet untold.

Stories Carved in Bark

The trees exclaimed, 'Get close, my friends!
I've tales to tell that never end!'
With circles deep and lines so grand,
They scratch their secrets in the sand.

A wise old oak with twists and turns,
Said, 'Listen closely, as the woodburns!
I've seen the weather change its tune,
And squirrels practicing afternoon!'

With every knot, a chuckle shared,
Of garden gnomes who thought they dared.
They tried to dance on summer's grass,
And ended up a silly ass.

In bark the lore of laughter thrived,
With stories carved and joy derived.
Each ring a wink, each shade a jest,
In nature's heart, we all are blessed.

The Rhythm of Nature's Embrace

In the park, a tree did dance,
With a squirrel in a funny trance.
He wore a hat made of bark,
As he twirled around, igniting the spark.

The flowers giggled, swayed in tune,
As bees buzzed like a crazy cartoon.
A bird tried to sing a jazz riff,
But its tone was more like a clumsy stiff.

Pine cones fell, like nature's confetti,
Landing on a rabbit, less than ready.
It hopped away, startled and quick,
While the crowd laughed, at the humor so slick.

Nature's stage, a laugh riot show,
Leaves were clapping, putting on a glow.
With every breeze, a new joke arose,
In this green paradise, mirth freely flows.

Dreams Clothed in Green

A little seed dreamed of being tall,
But tripped on roots; oh, what a fall!
With every sprout, it cracked a smile,
And made a friend in a worm, all the while.

The daisies giggled at the sun's bright beam,
Making shadows that danced, a funny theme.
A beetle tap-danced, its moves quite slick,
Spinning in circles, it made quite the trick.

The tall grass whispered secrets so loud,
To passing clouds, it felt so proud.
A gust of wind said, "Let's all take flight!"
But tangled branches turned glee into fright.

Yet in this grove, laughter is free,
As nature narrates its wild decree.
In dreams clothed in green, joy weaves like thread,
Reminding us all, to dance instead.

Beyond the Faded Leaves

Beyond the leaves of amber and gold,
Lies a tale of mischief, both loud and bold.
A chipmunk dressed in a tiny cape,
Swore to save acorns, it's quite the shape!

With a grand plan involving a stunt,
It leapt from branches, oh what a hunt!
But missed the mark, and landed rather near,
A startled cat, which filled it with fear.

The laughter echoed, humans' delight,
As the chipmunk scampered, out of sight.
"What a show!" the sparrows chirped in glee,
Nature's comedy, wild as can be.

So if you wander where tall trees stand,
Look for the antics, so well unplanned.
Beyond the faded leaves, humor takes flight,
And nature's stage is forever bright.

The Murmur of Twigs

The twigs whispered tales as shadows began,
Of a duck in a pond, who thought it a plan.
To host a ballet, with frogs in a row,
But their dancing? Ah, more like a show!

The frogs wore hats made of lily pads,
Swayed to the rhythm, while the pond truly had,
Ripples of laughter, from fish in the dark,
Who snickered and splashed, like a merry lark.

A turtle joined, with its slow, grand flair,
Tryna boogie, with elegance rare.
But slipped and flopped, creating a splash,
The audience gasped, then burst out in a crash!

Through the murmur of twigs, humor ran free,
In this quirky ballet, pure joy to see.
With nature's applause, the dance carried on,
In a world where laughter is never gone.

Moments in Green Growth

I saw a little sprout look up,
A worm just said, 'What's in your cup?'
The tree replied, 'Just morning dew,
But I'll share some with a friend like you!'

A leaf got tickled by a breeze,
It laughed and danced among the trees,
The sunlight winked, a playful glare,
Said, 'Grow up tall; it's fun out there!'

A beetle boasted, 'I can fly!'
But in the grass, it didn't try.
It took a leap and tumbled down,
And now it wears a leafy crown!

The flowers giggled, all in bloom,
'Why do the weeds always make room?'
They swayed and swirled in colors bright,
With cheeky grins, oh what a sight!

Ink of the Earth

A tiny mushroom wrote a play,
With gnomes and fairies in array.
The script was splattered with some mud,
As ants rehearsed, they slipped and thud!

The earthworm glared, 'That's not the line!'
The mushrooms laughed at their design.
'Let's rewrite this with a twist of fun,
And make the ending be a pun!'

A clumsy snail tried to join in,
With slippery trails, a messy win.
'No time for haste!' the trimmers cried,
But the snail just smirked and slipped with pride!

The grasslands cheered, their voices light,
'Let's bring on autumn, what a sight!'
With whispers tickled by the wind,
Let's start the tales, let laughter blend!

The Charm of New Growth

Buds popped up with a chit and chatter,
They giggled loud, 'What's the matter?'
A squirrel jumped, with nuts in tow,
He paused to watch the blossoms glow.

A daisy said, 'I'll tell a joke!'
The sun peeked through; it thought it spoke.
'To bloom or not? That's not the quest,
But how to grow? Now that's the jest!'

A bumblebee hummed to its tune,
'Let's all get busy; we'll dance by noon!'
The tulips twirled in rainbow hues,
While daisies laughed in cheerful views.

Through smiles and growth, we frolic free,
In this wild garden, come join the spree!
Nature's playground, bright and bold,
With stories of laughter waiting to unfold!

Voices of the Wild

The bushes whispered, 'Come and see,
A squirrel just tried to climb a tree!'
It missed a branch, went bouncing back,
Now it's hiding, its patience lacks!

Blades of grass sang sweetly low,
'There's a rabbit with a funny bow!'
He tripped and tumbled, oh what grace,
A hoppy dash turned into a race!

The flowers joined in, colors bright,
Telling tales of a comical plight.
'See that crow? He's bold and brash,
But watch him trip! A flapping crash!'

With laughter ringing through the air,
Nature's antics, beyond compare.
In every nook, a giggle hides,
Where joy and greenery coincide!

Whims of Wildflowers

Little daisies dance with glee,
When the wind whispers a tune, you see.
They giggle and sway, hey what a sight,
Trying to outrun the bugs in flight.

Tulips pose like they're on a catwalk,
Strutting their stuff, ready to talk.
But when the rain falls, they squeal and hide,
Only to emerge once the sun's at their side.

Bluebells chime with laughter, so bright,
Telling jokes to the bees, what a delight!
While marigolds boast of their sunny hue,
Saying, "Follow us! We know what to do!"

Each petal's a story, each leaf a song,
In the garden where flowers don't belong.
They remind us that life can be rather silly,
With plants that laugh, the world is always frilly.

The Heart of the Forest

In the woods where the squirrels play,
The trees tell tales in a rustling way.
A pine once claimed to touch the stars,
Yet it tripped on its roots and fell on the cars.

Moss gathers round like a fuzzy crew,
Critiquing the owls in their spectacles too.
"Whooo are you staring at?" they say with a scoff,
While the squirrels giggle, their acorns in scoff.

The raccoons have parties, their masks worn with pride,
They hoard all the snacks, it's quite a wild ride.
When the moon shines bright, they shimmy and sway,
Making forest frolics for the night and day.

All creatures gather, a whirling bit fun,
From foxes to rabbits, they play until done.
The heart of the forest beats loud with cheer,
Where laughter's the language that all critters hear.

Seasons of Renewal

In spring, the bunnies jump with delight,
They've forgotten their burrows, what a funny sight!
Daisies pop out, like old friends in town,
While the tulip brigade wears their best gown.

Summer brings sun and a picnic spree,
With ants marching in for the cake and tea.
The butterflies host the elaborate show,
While saying, "Greetings, do check out my glow!"

Autumn arrives with a whimsical flair,
Leaves swirling like dancers in the cool, crisp air.
Pumpkin jokes float as they hit the ground,
Each chuckle and giggle in the chill resound.

Winter rolls in with a blanket of white,
Snowflakes whisper stories deep into the night.
Critters all cozy in their tiny abodes,
Dreaming of spring and the laughter they've sowed.

Pathways of Green

Through the meadows, laughter does roam,
Each step a story, each blade a poem.
The grass tickles toes, it's a slippery ride,
With giggles exploding as they slide wide.

A path lined with daisies, a whimsical lane,
They chatter and chuckle, driving walkers insane.
"Watch your step!" they giggle, "It's slippery here,
You might trip on a leaf, then we'll have a cheer!"

Tall ferns offer shade, great hat wearers too,
While mushrooms make jokes that are quite out of view.
"Why did the toadstool sit by the tree?"
"Because it wanted some shade and a cup of green tea!"

On pathways of green where the fun never ends,
Nature's a clown with its mischievous bends.
With each little twist, every footfall it brings,
There's joy in the air, and the laughter just sings.

Awakening the Earth

Tiny leaves peek out in glee,
Waving hello to the busy bee.
Roots tickle below, oh so sly,
Whispering secrets to the sky.

Sneaky worms throw a dance,
While ants march by in a tiny prance.
A squirrel hops, clueless, quite funny,
Stepping on petals, not for money!

Earthworms giggle, playing at night,
Planning a party when it's bright.
Under the moon, they wiggle and spin,
A worm disco? Let the fun begin!

With each breeze, a story unfolds,
Of droopy flowers and ruffled folds.
Laughter echoes through nature's chat,
As winds blow tales of this and that.

Silent Growth

In stillness, young shoots stretch and yawn,
While busy grasshoppers plot at dawn.
With a giggle, each petal curls,
Nature's way of throwing swirls.

The sun peeks in with a cheeky grin,
Scattering warmth where the fun begins.
Roots having meetings in the cool, dark,
Planning a heist—a veggie park!

Beneath the soil, where whispers play,
Tiny creatures have their own ballet.
Fungal fungi spin tales with flair,
While turtles nod, ponder life's rare air.

As time goes by, the laughter grows,
In the land where no one knows.
Nature chuckles, a silent cheer,
At the joyful scenes far and near.

Circle of Roots

Beneath the surface, a party resides,
Roots mingle around like joyful guides.
They crack jokes in a wormy tone,
Swaying together, never alone.

A squirrel trips, laughs fill the ground,
As acorns roll and tumble around.
Roots whisper tales over grapevine,
Of silly games and the best sunshine.

With each twist, a funny dance,
Roots compete in a groovy trance.
"Did you see that twig tumble down?
It cracked a joke and made me clown!"

So many friends below the earth,
Sharing laughter, for what it's worth.
In the circle, joy takes flight,
Roots weaving humor, pure delight.

Stories Beneath the Bark

Within the bark, tales take a twist,
Of mischievous critters you can't resist.
A woodpecker tells a raucous lie,
While beetles chuckle and stroll on by.

The sap drips down in a sticky line,
"Who drew the map? Oh, that's just fine!"
Rabbits giggle at the wood's tall tales,
While ants debate their wiggling trails.

Each ring of growth tells stories bright,
Of funny happenings through day and night.
"Did you hear the tale of the tree who sang?
It missed each note, and oh, what a clang!"

So listen closely when shadows fall,
To the giggles and whispers that fill the hall.
Nature's a friend with laughter to share,
Inside the bark, where stories flare.

Whispers of Green

In the garden, seeds do chatter,
They gossip 'bout the rain that splatters.
'Did you see the squirrel's silly dance?
He thinks he's part of this green expanse!'

Leaves tickle branches with cheery jokes,
While daisies giggle at the silly folks.
'Oh, look! The beetle is stuck in a loop,
Bouncing around like a clumsy troop!'

Sunbeams shine their spotlight bright,
As plants perform in sheer delight.
'Where's the audience?' the tulips cry,
'Just us and the butterfly up in the sky!'

Roots do wiggle in underground glee,
As they plan a surprise for the big old tree.
'His bark is tough, but we'll make him laugh,
With our secret party and our leafy craft!'

Beneath the Canopy

Beneath the trees, our shadows play,
Where little critters roam and sway.
Squirrels joke that they're acrobats,
Flipping through branches like sunny brats!

'Have you met my friend the chipmunk, dear?
He thinks he's the next big pioneer!'
Worms wiggle in their wiggle dance,
Trying to catch a break — or just a chance!

A piglet wandered in looking lost,
'Why is the grass so sweet, at what cost?'
The rabbits giggled with carrot delight,
'Eat up, buddy, it's the best tonight!'

In the shade, they all find their beat,
Singing 'round with little feet.
Laughter echoes from root to bloom,
While the forest shakes off the dusty gloom!

Roots of Tomorrow

Roots are plotting with a belly laugh,
'Let's stretch our limbs for a photo graph!'
But the daisies shout, 'Not so fast,
Last time you won — we fell on our grass!'

Each root wriggles, a sneaky plot,
'How about we prank the lilac spot?'
With a tickle here and a nudge there,
The flowers giggle as they toss in the air!

The sun looks down and cracks a grin,
As the squirrels plot their cheeky win.
Who needs a crown? Let's wear the dirt,
Roots in a riot, oh, what a spurt!

Dig deep, they chant, 'For fun's sweet sake,
Tomorrow's tales are ours to make!'
With muddy hands and laughter loud,
They vow to be brave and very proud!

Growth Beneath the Surface

Beneath the ground, it's a lively race,
Where moles are ninjas, just in case!
A tune of roots, they sway to the beat,
Dancing to the rhythm of wormy feet!

'Hey, buddy mole! How's the underground?
Do you hear the giggles all around?'
Moles pop up with a cheeky grin,
'The gardening gossip spreads like wind!'

Fungi cheerfully join the fun,
'We're the party mushrooms under the sun!'
Riddles and rhymes they all recite,
Creating a kingdom hidden from sight!

With each new shoot, there's a giggle burst,
For growth beneath is a whimsical thirst.
Nature's jesters, in soil's embrace,
Crafting stories that time cannot erase!

Under the Watchful Skies

A tiny sprout with dreams so big,
It wishes to dance like a jubilant jig.
With roots that wiggle, it feels so spry,
Hey, look at me! I'm reaching for the sky!

With each raindrop, it giggles with glee,
Singing out loud, 'Oh, look at me!'
A bird flies by, says, 'You're quite bold!'
The little sprout shivers, but never gets cold.

Worms come to chat, 'You're a curious sight!'
They share their tales of the day and night.
The sprout just chuckles, 'I'm just getting started!'
In the garden of dreams, it feels quite hearted.

Under the watchful skies, life is a treat,
With friends all around, and sunshine so sweet.
It stretches higher, with laughter in tow,
In the playground of gardens, it steals the show.

The Language of New Life

A whisper of green in a world full of grey,
A button-nosed bud joins in on the play.
As sunlight tickles, it giggles on cue,
'This soil is cozy—who knew it was true?'

With ants marching by, it gives a sly grin,
'Hello, little critters! Let's hang out and win!'
The ladybug winks, 'Life's quite absurd,
You'll find your rhythm, just listen: no word!'

Rain falls like laughter from clouds up above,
While the breeze dances by, spreading some love.
'Nonsense is wisdom,' the sprout starts to sing,
With snickers and squeals, it's a laugh-off fling.

The melody hums through the roots deep below,
Speaking in whispers that nobody knows.
In the chatter of blooms, it discovers delight,
New life speaks in fun, oh, what a sight!

Buds of Resilience

Little green buds on a perilous path,
Face storms with a grin, who can do the math?
'You call that a gust?' they chuckle and sway,
Daring the wind to come play, come play!

With friends by their sides, leaning to cheer,
'We're tough as nails, no need to fear!'
The raindrops pelt down like silly old foes,
But the buds laugh louder as their laughter grows.

Beneath the soil, the worms start to plot,
Turning the dirt into a warm, cozy spot.
'Just a few more inches, we'll break through the ground,
Then the real fun begins—oh, what joy will be found!'

With sunny faces and brave little hearts,
The buds wiggle upwards, embracing new starts.
Standing up tall, they take on the day,
Being resilient in every funny way.

In the Shadow of Giants

Growing up small in a forest of tall,
The giants above, with their grandeur enthrall.
'Don't mind us,' say the oaks, with a wink,
'We were once sproutlings! Go on, just think!'

The little ones giggle, 'We're just biding time,
Soon we'll be tall, and then we'll rhyme!'
The pines share their tales of great heights and wins,
'Enjoy the small stuff; that's how joy begins!'

In the shade, they throw dance parties at dusk,
To the sounds of the breeze and the rustle of musk.
'Shake it, little buddy! Move as you please!'
They jiggle and giggle, swaying with ease.

With laughter so loud, it rumbles the ground,
They celebrate life, with joy that surrounds.
In the shadow of giants, their hearts are alive,
With big dreams and fun, oh, how they thrive!

Beneath the Old Oak

In the shade of the grand old oak,
A squirrel cracked a nut and spoke,
"Have you heard the latest joke?
The acorn's lost, and that's no hoax!"

Underneath the leafy crown,
A rabbit danced and twirled around,
"I lost my hat, it fell right down,
Now I'm the silly bunny clown!"

The woodpecker laughed with beak to wood,
"Why can't trees knit? It's understood!"
The leaves just rustled, mischief stirred,
"Because they always twist and brooded!"

As time went on, they shared their cheer,
With stories swapped from ear to ear,
Beneath the oak, jokes drew them near,
In nature's laughter, there's no fear!

New Life Among Giants

A tiny sprout stood proud and tall,
Amidst the giants, it felt small,
It wobbled once, it slipped and fell,
Then giggled loud, it rang the bell!

The towering trees groaned with delight,
"Look at that sprout, what a funny sight!"
They whispered tales of strength and height,
Yet shrunk in fear of a bug's great bite!

The sapling grinned, a daring deed,
"I'll grow my leaves, I'll plant a seed!"
"Branches may bend, but hearts will lead,
Among the mighty, you can find speed!"

With every push, it grew some more,
While legends around it started to soar,
Among the giants, it found the core,
Laughter echoed, forever in store.

A Symphony of Growth

In the forest played a merry tune,
As sprouts began their lively croon,
"Who knew growth could spark such glee?"
Even the roots joined in, you see!

The daisies tapped with rhythmic flair,
While ferns swayed, bouncing in the air,
"Let's have a party, we don't care!"
The moss just shrugged, it had no hair!

A chipmunk danced with acorns bright,
He twirled around with pure delight,
"Let's celebrate our leafy plight!
Growth sings! Dance under moonlight!"

As moonbeams poured like sweet sunshine,
The forest echoed, a vibrant line,
The symphony of growth divine,
Made every leaf and critter align!

The Promise of Seasons

The springtime brought a laughing breeze,
The daisies turned, danced with ease,
"Hey look! There's sunshine, yes indeed!
Let's swap our jokes and plant a seed!"

Summer followed, with fun galore,
The ants marched in, a knock on door,
"We've come to party, who wants more?
We'll dance till night, forget the chore!"

Then autumn strolled with colors bright,
The leaves turned red, a dazzling sight,
"Let's have a feast, oh what a bite!
Cornucopia! Hooray for the night!"

When winter whispers, cold and clear,
A cozy laugh, with holiday cheer,
"Let's bundle up, embrace the year!
Seasons change, but joy stays near!"

Emergence under Canopy

In a world of green, things go awry,
A squirrel's dance, caught in the sky.
A leaf does a twirl, says, "Look at me!"
While the roots chuckle with glee.

A tiny worm winks, with a wiggle and twist,
"Here comes the rain, I hope I exist!"
Grabbing his coat made of dew and mud,
He sails through puddles, oh what a flood!

The daisies gossip, their petals aflutter,
Sneaking around like they're on a taunter.
"Did you hear? The gardener tripped, oh dear!"
With roots and leaves, they share a sneer.

But when the sun shines, they throw a ball,
Each little flower joining the brawl.
Dancing in light, they twinkle and sway,
In the canopy, they've found their play.

When Buds Begin to Bloom

Buds burst open with a hilarious cheer,
A bumblebee stumbles, takes flight with fear.
"I'm not a flower!" it buzzed with a frown,
As petals giggled, floating down.

A bug in a hat played a flute made of grass,
As ants strutted by, in a fancy class.
"Look at us dance!" the daisies all shout,
While the young buds spin, twirl, and pout.

The tulips agreed, "We must steal the show!"
While thinking of pranks they could probably sow.
But a gust blew through, and petals did rain,
"Now we're a confetti parade!" they exclaim.

But bloom-time is quick, so they laugh and they cheer,
Determined to spread fun till the end of the year.
Each color a jester, bright in their hue,
Under the sun, hilarity grew!

The Soft Awakening

Awake in the morn, with a yawn, what a sight,
A snail with a shell says, "I'm ready to bite!"
His breakfast, a leaf, is the softest of treats,
"Forget your cereal, this veggie's the feat!"

Beneath the bright sun, fun starts to bloom,
A pillow of moss becomes everyone's room.
"Let's have a party!" chirps a young thrush,
With worms for dessert in a leafy lush hush.

The ladybugs danced, wearing spots like their crowns,
"Best party of the year!" they said in their gowns.
Branches joined in, conducting the band,
While shadows crept in to lend a soft hand.

The sun began to set, with a wink and a grin,
Flashing their colors, the fun must begin!
So every wee creature, from root to the sky,
Sang songs of the night, with a bright, happy sigh.

Underneath the Surface

In the depths where giggles run free as a stream,
The worms set up camp, plotting their dream.
"Who knew dirt could bring so much cheer?"
They chuckle and wiggle, without any fear.

A mysterious toad croaks a joke quite absurd,
"What kind of music do roots prefer?"
The audience whispers, with bated delight,
"The best 'soil' music—roots that feel right!"

Beneath the sagebrush, where shadows all play,
The critters convene at the end of the day.
"Tomorrow's picnic, don't forget the spread!"
"Let's stack all the leaves, and lay on the bed!"

And as darkness cloaked, they nestled with glee,
The laughter of critters, a soft, joyous spree.
In the soil, they dream of the fun yet to come,
With nature as their stage, they gleefully hum.

The Poetics of Possibility

In a garden of dreams, I tend the weeds,
A carrot in a hat, plotting grand deeds.
With radish in boots, and celery in pants,
They dance and they jig, oh what a romance.

The flowers gossip in dazzling delight,
Telling tales of mischief, from morning to night.
A pumpkin named Gary won't stay in his patch,
He's sneaking off daily to pick up a batch.

A zucchini with stripes has a flair for the show,
She struts through the garden like she's in a flow.
While beans with their pals throw a wiggle parade,
In this wacky place, every inch is displayed.

So here in this plot, where the odd becomes norm,
Nature's own circus will always transform.
With laughter and giggles, we'll cover the place,
Making poetics of future, in soil's warm embrace.

Sowing Seeds of Tomorrow

Not an acorn, but a pebble I threw,
Hoping for splendor, or a tree maybe two.
But the tree that emerged was more like a toy,
Swinging and spinning like a wild little boy.

The flowers were puzzled, the neighbors all gawked,
As the carrots held meetings, and radishes talked.
They plotted the course of their veggie domain,
A kingdom of laughter, where silliness reigned.

In rows of bright colors, the games came alive,
A cabbage that giggled, a daisy that thrives.
Potatoes played soccer, and onions held court,
Each day brought a ruckus, a merry old sort.

So planting a seed is a journey quite grand,
With laughter and joy spilling over the land.
Each little sprout tells a tale of delight,
Sowing tomorrow, under skies ever bright.

The Allure of the Unseen

Underneath the soil, a ruckus unfolds,
With whispers and giggles, and roots making folds.
They've founded a club, calling it 'The Roots,'
Where dreams are all shared, and nobody hoots.

A shy little sprout claims he's invisible,
But wormy friends shout, "Oh, that's just impossible!"
With laughter, they dive in the soft, cool earth,
Celebrating the magic of each tiny birth.

Mice tap their feet to a rhythm of fun,
While mushrooms groove under the light of the sun.
They hatch wild ideas—sky-high adventures,
In this world of wonder, they break all the censures.

So listen quite closely, to tales underground,
For the unseen wonders are waiting to be found.
In every sprout's heart, a secret or two,
Inviting you in to explore something new.

Lullabies of the Woods

The leaves start to gossip as the sun sinks low,
Singing sweet lullabies to the trees down below.
Squirrels wear pajamas, all snug in their nests,
While chipmunks recount their most hilarious quests.

Bunnies hold parties 'neath the soft moonlight,
With carrots in hand, all feeling just right.
The birds are the band, chirping melodies rare,
As fireflies twinkle, filling up the night air.

The hedgehogs rock slowly, in a wavy embrace,
While whispers of laughter float into the space.
Each rustle and giggle wraps round like a hug,
As nature hums softly, sweet bedtime's a drug.

So drift into slumber, sweet dreams take their flight,
In this realm of the woods, where all feels just right.
The lullabies linger till dawn's early breeze,
In the silliness of night, under towering trees.

The Treetop Tales

In a forest bright and gay,
A squirrel lost its way to play.
It climbed a tree, oh what a sight!
But now it's stuck, oh what a fright!

A parrot squawked, 'Get down, my friend!'
The squirrel said, 'I'll climb till the end!
With views like this, who needs the ground?'
And on a branch, he spun around!

A woodpecker laughed, tapping the bark,
'You came up high, but no way to park!'
The squirrel shrugged, with a cheeky grin,
'Guess I'll just stay and enjoy the spin!'

Then all the animals gathered near,
To cheer the squirrel, oh what a cheer!
He finally leapt with all his might,
And landed safely, oh what a sight!

Portraits of Resilience

A tiny seed with dreams so bold,
Buried deep, but not too cold.
It poked its head, in sunlight's beam,
And laughed, 'Oh look, I'm living the dream!'

The wind blew strong, it swayed and danced,
With every gust, it took a chance.
'Like a kite, I soar so high,'
It jingled leaves, 'Watch me fly!'

A curious bunny passed by fast,
Said, 'Hold on tight, you'll be outclassed!'
The seedling grinned, 'Just wait and see,
I'll be a tree, then climb with glee!'

And though it trembled, it stood up straight,
For every storm, it learned to wait.
Soon roots grew deep, branches spread wide,
A towering tree with joy and pride!

Nurtured in the Light

A caterpillar hung from a tree,
Complaining, 'Why's this leaf not free?'
It munched and grumbled, day and night,
Till sunlight winked, 'Hey! You're alright!'

'What's that glow? Why the big fuss?'
Asked the worm, 'Was it something I discussed?'
The sun just beamed, 'You'll see it soon,
The light will help you be a boon!'

With a flip and twist, it wiggled about,
Said, 'Maybe this is what it's about!'
And when it wrapped, snug in a cocoon,
It dreamed of skies and playing tunes.

Then one fine day, it broke the shell,
Flapping wings as it rang the bell.
A butterfly laughed, 'Look at me glide!'
'Thanks, little sun, for this wild ride!'

Under the Shade of New Dreams

In a garden of giggles, a flower grew,
With petals so bright, of every hue.
Said to a bee, 'You buzz so sweet!'
'Join me in dance, let's call it a treat!'

The bee spun round like a spinning top,
Bouncing off blooms, it simply could not stop!
'Under the sun, we'll have some fun,
With pollen and nectar, we'll never be done!'

The flower giggled, 'Let's paint the sky!'
Mixing colors, oh, they were sly!
While daisies chuckled, proud of their cheer,
Even the thorns felt welcome here.

And as the sun dipped, glowing rosy bright,
The garden whispered, 'What a delight!'
For even in shadows, joy can be found,
Under the shade, dreams spin around!

A Leaf's Journey

A little leaf fell from a tree,
He said, "Oh me, oh my, how free!"
He twirled and danced with all his might,
Until he landed on a cat's head, what a sight!

The cat just blinked, quite confused,
"Why is this green thing so amused?"
The leaf just chuckled, feeling spry,
"I'm just enjoying this wonderous high!"

He rode the wind, flying 'round,
Flew past a dog digging in the ground.
The dog barked up, "What's that in the sky?"
"A leaf with a dream! Oh my, oh my!"

Through parks and gardens he played all day,
Came winter's chill, and he lost his way.
But he just laughed, it's been quite the show!
"I'll come back again, just you wait and grow!"

The Seed's Quiet Dream

A tiny seed dreamed in the dirt,
"One day I won't be just a shirt!"
He wanted to sprout, reach for the sun,
But first, he had to have some fun!

He wiggles and giggles with roots so shy,
While worms around him say, "Oh my!"
He chats with ants about life so grand,
"I'm just a seed, but I have a plan!"

With rain's gentle tap, he felt quite bright,
"Almost there, I can feel the light!"
But then a hungry bird swooped low,
"Not so fast!" cried the seed, "I'm not ready to go!"

His friends in the soil cheered him on,
"Stay strong, little sprout, until the dawn!"
With dreams and laughter, he held his ground,
And soon enough, he'd be glory-bound!

Tales from the Forest Floor

On the forest floor, where the creatures roam,
A snail told tales of a life far from home.
"Just yesterday I tried to race a hare,
But he left me in dirt, so I went and had a pear!"

A wise old frog croaked, "That's a swell tale!
I've hopped around and ridden the gale.
But eating flies, oh what a pain,
They stick to my tongue like a bee in rain!"

A squirrel chimed in with a nut in his paws,
"I climb all the trees; I've no time for flaws!
But I swear, one day, I'll get that acorn,
And when I do, I'll be the king, I'm reborn!"

The forest giggled with leaves in the breeze,
"Let's all enjoy life, with laughter and ease!
For every tale spun in the dark or the light,
Makes the forest a stage, oh what a delight!"

Hopes Hidden in Soil

In the rich, dark soil where secrets lie,
The dreams of tomorrow are reaching for sky.
A little old worm wiggled with glee,
"Shh! Don't tell them, but I'm planting a tree!"

He gathered up whispers from roots all around,
And with a quick twist, he dug in the ground.
"My leafy friends, dreams are here to stay,
Let's sprout up together, let's shout hooray!"

And all of a sudden, a flower gave a shout,
"Hey, what's this fuss? Let me see, what's about!"
With laughter in petals it swayed in delight,
"Join our grand party, from day into night!"

So deep in the earth, with giggles and songs,
The hopes of the future grow right where it belongs.
With fun in the roots, they all settled in,
And awaited the sun with a great big grin!

The Gentle Rise

In a garden, tiny sprouts play,
Whispering secrets in the sun's ray.
They tickle the toes of passing bees,
Laughing with leaves in the soft breeze.

One little bud wore a leaf hat,
Pretending to be a wise old cat.
The others giggled, "What a sight!"
And danced around till the evening light.

A worm joined in with a funny jig,
"Look at me, I'm not that big!"
They twirled and spun on the fresh grass,
Creating laughter that none could surpass.

As stars began to twinkle above,
They sang to the moon, full of love.
The garden echoed with their delight,
A playful tale under the night.

Flourishing Futures

Beneath the soil, they dream and snooze,
Imagining branches, bright and blue hues.
"What if I grow with a cupcake twist?"
"Oh, what fun it is to be kissed!"

Their ambitions are grand; one wants to boast,
"I'll be the tallest, I'll be your host!"
But the tiny green couldn't keep a straight face,
"Let's party first; we'll win the race!"

They flirt with the sun, stretch to the sky,
While ants march by with a curious eye.
"Are you a tree or just playing tricks?"
"Both," they giggle, giving pokey kicks.

From acorns to dreams, together they chase,
Telling tall tales in their playful space.
With roots that wiggle and leaves that dance,
Every sprout knows it's a silly romance.

Green Silhouettes

Little green shadows, they peek and poke,
"Is that the sun or an old oak joke?"
With blades of grass acting like the crowd,
The giggles rise up, playful and loud.

A sprout named Timmy wears a proud grin,
"I'll grow a branch that will sweep you in!"
But Sally said, "With a twist like mine,
I'll have the best roots, looking divine!"

They play in the soil, making mud pies,
With glee in their hearts, reaching for the skies.
"Can we stick together in this green parade?"
"With twigs in a row, let's blend and invade!"

The world above is silly and bright,
As they giggle beneath the moonlight.
Every shadow holds a tale so sweet,
Of laughter and joy from their tiny feet.

The Unfolding Narrative

In patches of green, stories unfold,
Of raindrops that dance and leaves that scold.
There's Tucker the twig, with dreams so tall,
He sways and whispers, "I'll never fall!"

A berry bird swoops down to tease,
"Got any secrets or silly keys?"
They share a chuckle; everything is fun,
For tales of growth have only begun.

With every gust, they do a dance,
Twisting and turning, not missing a chance.
"I want to grow feathers and fly in a race!"
"Only if you can land in a pancake place!"

When dusk draws near, they gather in kin,
With a blanket of stars coloring their skin.
These whispers of joy in the wooden glen,
Echo the laughter of little green friends.

Fertile Whispers

A tiny twig with dreams so grand,
Wants to dance, but can't quite stand.
It wiggles and jigs, a leafy delight,
Shaking with laughter from morning to night.

The soil chuckles, a mischievous grin,
Says, "Grow up fast, let the fun begin!"
With roots so eager and leaves a-flutter,
It whispers to bugs, "Hey, come have some butter!"

The sun beams down, a spotlight bright,
"Plant your jokes, it's open mic night!"
The little sprout, with humor unbound,
Tells tales of worms that dance in the ground.

And as clouds giggle, they sprinkle some cheer,
"Don't worry, dear sprout, your pals will be near!"
With a puff of air, the laughter takes flight,
Thus a fun-filled forest springs into sight.

Heartbeats of the Earth

In the soil, a heartbeat quick,
A little sprout planning a trick.
"I'll tickle the toes of unsuspecting ants,
And make them do the silliest dance!"

The grass nods along with a swaying grin,
"Don't forget to invite the bugs in!"
They form a band with a leaf for a drum,
Playing catchy tunes that make everyone hum.

A butterfly joins, flapping in rhyme,
"We'll paint the world with laughter and time!"
The disco beneath the vast blue dome,
Turns the forest floor into a true home.

And when the night falls with twinkling stars,
They giggle at shadows, sharing their scars.
In the heartbeats of Earth, a melody sways,
While tiny sprouts dance through the silly days.

The Tender Embrace of Rain

A drop of rain with a tickle and thrill,
Whispers to plants, "I'm here for a chill!"
They stretch out their leaves, in glee they sing,
"Come dance with us, let's feel the zing!"

The puddles form pools for splish-splash fun,
With frogs in tuxedos, ready to run.
They hop and they skip, a wet gala of glee,
The rain, the DJ, makes them all free!

Oh what a show, in a downpour's embrace,
The plants get soggy, but wear smiles on their face.
Mud pies aplenty, squelching around,
Laughter erupts from the playful ground.

So raise up your roots, let the fun rain down,
In a world of puddles, let's dance all around!
With splashes and giggles, let joy stay afloat,
Together we'll sing in our watery boat!

Echoes of a Green Dawn

Morning light tickles the leaves awake,
As whispers of green begin to shake.
A frog croaks first, with a mighty bold tune,
While snails slide in, joyfully immune.

"Time for the breakfast of sunshine and dew!"
Says the ladybug, with her polka-dot crew.
They gather to nibble on sweet morning rays,
While giggling and jiggling in wondrous displays.

The grass tickles toes in a soft light breeze,
Each blade a comedian, bringing you to knees.
"What did one weed say to the other, my friend?"
"Let's shake up the garden, go wild without end!"

With laughter as the anthem, sprouts burst forth bright,
Echoes of giggles dance through the daylight.
In this symphony green, where joy starts to blend,
We find our connection, where nature's our friend.

The Language of Leaves

Green whispers flutter, oh so sly,
Tickling the air as passersby.
Leafy lingo, do you believe?
Tales of squirrels, just take your leave!

Caught in a breeze, they salsa and sway,
A dance-off between the oak and the bay.
Unruly branches take silly bows,
While the grass giggles and wonders how.

Gossipy twigs exchanging secrets,
Confetti of pollen, their light-hearted feats.
Breezes shake hands with every green head,
Nutty jokes from the roots, often misled!

So next time you wander, stop and just see,
The chuckling foliage waiting for thee.
Listen for laughter, it's all in full leaf,
Nature's own comedy, beyond belief!

Unwritten Tales in the Bark

Rugged surfaces, like novels untold,
Each groove a chapter, a history bold.
Trees chuckle softly, inked in their grain,
Reciting their lives in a whimsical vein.

Caterpillars penning their memoirs in haste,
While woodpeckers drum-up some comic taste.
A bug-scribbled story, a bark-borne delight,
Of parties at dusk—what a silly sight!

The wise old trunk, with gnarled, knotted grin,
Sipping on sunlight, inviting you in.
Secrets exchanged with a wink and a nod,
A comic-book forest, where laughter's the God!

So pause and peruse these loopy tales,
Of beetles in tuxedos and ants in gales.
Nature's great scribbles, oh what a laugh,
Unwritten stories, our green photograph!

Spinning Dreams in Sunlight

In the dappled light, the sun's a trickster,
Spinning bright yarns, each twist a twister.
A playful hand weaves shadows and rays,
Crafting warm fantasies that dance and amaze.

Glowing dandelions puff dreams in the air,
Wishing on seeds, if only we dare.
Butterflies buzz as they share their delight,
In this tapestry woven from morning to night.

The laughter of blossoms, such sweet, merry bells,
Echoes of stories, like whimsical spells.
A breeze brushes past, tickling nearby,
As dreams spin in sunlight, up to the sky.

So frolic with filters of magic and glee,
Join the round dance, breathe in the spree.
Catch the warm humor of life in a twirl,
And let sunlight's laughter make your heart whirl!

Harmony of the New

Tiny shoots stretch with innocent zeal,
In a world that's fresh, so surreal.
With every new leaf, there's a cartoonish flair,
They giggle and wiggle, claiming their share.

New blooms are singing, oh what a song!
To the rhythm of spring, where all things belong.
Flowering friendships, buds sharing a jest,
In a garden of giggles, they dance and jest.

The world is a playground, soft soil and cheer,
With roots splaying dreams beneath, ever near.
Nature's own orchestra, conducting with glee,
The harmony of antics, wild and free.

So join in the laughter of all things anew,
Where seedlings are pitching, and humor grows too.
With each little sprout, make way for some fun,
The joyful beginnings have only begun!

Celestial Roots

In a garden where the stars play,
Tiny seeds plot their hilarious way.
Whispers of sun, tickles from rain,
Dance with the winds, driving them insane.

They giggle as they stretch towards the sky,
Huddled together, how high can we fly?
As worms wiggle by with a wink and a grin,
They toss in some dirt, and the chaos begins.

Jokes about heights shared without care,
Branches all tangled, tangled in hair.
Roots in a race for the best underground seat,
All while avoiding a pesky old beet.

Under the moonlight, they twist and shout,
"We're not so small; we're big, there's no doubt!"
Laughter resounding 'neath the bright, starry dome,
In each little sprout, there's a giggly gnome.

Cradled by Earth

Nestled deep in the cozy ground,
Giggles bubble up without a sound.
With a tickle from roots ensuring they're stout,
They whisper the tales that make you pout.

Worms wearing hats want to join in the fun,
"Make room for us, we want to run!"
But sprouts flip and flop, saying, "Not so fast,
We're busy, dear worms, we've a fun spell to cast!"

Ants form a line, a parade on a quest,
Holding tiny banners, they think they're the best.
But the sprigs roll their eyes, having heard all their chat,
"We're the stars of this show, just look at that hat!"

The sun pokes a joke, "Did you hear that last pun?"
And the seedlings respond, "No, come tell us for fun!"
In the earth's warm embrace, what a wacky scene,
With nature's own laughter, it's an uproarous routine.

The Silent Awakening

Awake from their dreams, the buds take a peek,
Feeling the sunlight as they start to speak.
"What did we miss while we lay on the ground?"
"Another funny tale or two might be found!"

They nudge one another with leaves full of glee,
"What challenges await? Let's go wait and see!"
With roots in a tangle, they giggle with pride,
"Let's venture above where the silliness hides!"

But a sudden raindrop plops, causing a splash,
Jumping with joy, the greens start to dash.
"Catch me if you can!" they gleefully sing,
As droplets turn dancers, making them wing.

And the moon, peeking out, rolls its eyes at the show,
"Nature's comedians, always stealing the glow."
With laughter echoing beneath the sky bright,
Each bud tells a story in pure joy and delight.

Chronicles of a Budding World

In a realm where the petals tell tales with flair,
A chorus of sprouts serenades the air.
Each bloom keeps a secret, a giggle's delight,
As bees buzz like comedians, flying in sight.

"Watch out for the hedgehog!" a sprout freely shouts,
"He gets cranky and rolls when he pouts!"
Laughter erupts from the blossoms all round,
Turning whispers of earth into giggles abound.

They share notes with the butterflies flitting about,
"Life is so fun, there's no room for doubt!"
As shadows grow long, and the stars twinkle bright,
The petals snicker softly, wishing to unite.

With humor like sunlight that lifts every heart,
These chronicles spark joy as true works of art.
In a world where the stories of flora unfold,
Life's silly antics never get old.

www.ingramcontent.com/pod-product-compliance
Lightning Source LLC
Chambersburg PA
CBHW071816160426
43209CB00003B/104